"How would you like to g
encouraging letter from God?
from God. She *knows* that God directed you to read
these letters!"

— SID ROTH, HOST, *IT'S SUPERNATURAL!*

"Ana Werner is a prophetess who walks in integrity,
truth, and love. Where does that flow from? — her
sacred times with God. She always shares deep insights
of wisdom and purity. I love and endorse Ana Werner."

— PATRICIA KING, AUTHOR, TV HOST, MINISTER

"Ana has done it again! She has heard the heart of the
Father and passed His feelings of Love to you! These
prophetic revelations show you who you are to the
Father and who the Father wants to be to you. Get
ready...you're getting ready to know Jesus and the
Father in ways you never knew before!!"

— PASTOR TONY KEMP, PRESIDENT OF *THE
APOSTOLIC COUNSELING AND TRAINING SERVICES*

"Ana Werner's latest book, *Letters to the Unforgotten,* is
such a beautiful, deep well of revelation and
encouragement for you that will usher you into some of
the deepest encounters with the Lord's heart for you.
His voice comforting, healing, strengthening and
empowering you. This book is an invitation into a
deeper realm of intimacy with your Beloved."

— LANA VAWSER, FOUNDER OF *LANA VAWSER
MINISTRIES*

Letters to the Unforgotten

ISBN: 978-1-7353469-5-3

A Publication of Tall Pine Books

| | *tallpinebooks.com*

*Printed in the United States of America

Letters to the Unforgotten

God's prophetic love letters to You

ANA WERNER

Volume 1

To my dear aunt Jean. Your unfailing love and support in my life, has meant the world to me.

CONTENTS

1 | I'VE GOT YOU

"From the moment I formed you in Heaven,
I destined you to be great.
Nothing is standing in your way
But fear itself.
Fear is trying to hold you back,
But I created you to live this exhilarating life with Me.
I've been with you from the very beginning.
I've never left you.
No one can do what I'm calling you to.
With all your quirks,
All your life experiences,
You were made for this.
Come on and take the plunge!
Trust Me.
I've got you!"

"I am doing something brand new, something unheard of. Even now it sprouts and grows and matures. Don't you perceive it? I will make a way in the wilderness and open up flowing streams in the desert."

— Isaiah 43:19, TPT

"I see you
in this moment of pain.
I see you.
I'm here my child. I'm really here.
I've never left you. I've always been pursuing you.
Even in this moment when it feels like I am far off or distant,
Would you believe that I am not?
I am your strength.
Come lean against My chest today.
I am here!"

*"Out of my deep anguish and pain I prayed, and God, you helped me
as a father. You came to my rescue and broke open the way into a
beautiful and broad place."*

— Psalm 118:5, TPT

3 | LET ME CARRY YOU

"It's time to let it go.
Come on over here,
My son, my daughter.
Let Me wash you afresh again.
Give Me your disappointments.
Hand over the burdens;
Hand over the pressures
You are feeling right now.
Let Me take care of them.
Let Me carry you."

*"For I know the thoughts that I think toward you, says the Lord,
thoughts of peace and not of evil, to give you a future and a hope."*

— JEREMIAH 29:11, NKJV

"Won't you let Me in a little deeper?
Let Me into those deep vulnerable places.
I see all your insecurities,
Your weaknesses,
The places you don't want anyone to see.
I see it all.
I still love you.
Don't you see?
It's time to lay down your walls.
In your weakened state,
You will find Me."

"Will you trust Him because His strength is great? Or will you leave your labor to Him?"

— JOB 39:11, NKJV

5 | COME TAKE MY HAND

"Let My peace invade your day.
Take a step back from life's happenings.
Come walk with Me in the Garden.
Here I am.
Come take My hand and find Me again.
Look at the way I so tenderly care for each of My flowers here.
Don't you think I care for you
More than that?
Walk with Me.
Just stay a little longer here.
Come take My hand,
Let Me fill you with peace."

"Listen, my radiant one—if you ever lose sight of me, just follow in my footsteps where I lead my lovers. Come with your burdens and cares. Come to the place near the sanctuary of my shepherds."

— SONG OF SONGS 1:8, TPT

"Don't hold back!
I have given you a voice that's strong
And meant to be heard.
Don't let intimidation overtake you.
Don't allow anyone to poison your mind,
Thinking you are less.
You were created to shine!
You will not be shaken."

"When you walk, your steps will not be hindered, and when you run, you will not stumble."

— PROVERBS 4:12, NKJV

7 | SOAR AGAIN!

"No one defines you, but Me.
No one can put you in a box.
You are free.
You are really free!
It's time to break out of the prison
that the enemy has tried to hold you in.
May your wings be unclipped,
Unrestrained.
It's time to soar again!"

"For you have not received a spirit of slavery leading to fear again, but you have received a spirit of adoption as sons and daughters by which we cry out, 'Abba! Father!' The Spirit Himself testifies with our spirit that we are children of God…"

— ROMANS 8:15-16, NASB

"Find Me.
Slow down
And find Me.
I'm not so far, I'm right here.
I've always been speaking to you,
Sometimes even in a whisper.
Lay down your projects,
Lay down your tasks.
Let's drink in the sunshine and fresh air together.
Find Me again."

"Who, then, ascends into the presence of the Lord? And who has the privilege of entering into God's Holy Place? Those who are clean— whose works and ways are pure, whose hearts are true and sealed by the truth, those who never deceive, whose words are sure. They will receive the Lord's blessing and righteousness given by the Savior- God. They will stand before God, for they seek the pleasure of God's face, the God of Jacob. Pause in His presence."

— PSALM 24:3-6, TPT

"It's time to get your joy back!
I remember when you used to really
Enjoy life.
It's like you would sit on a swing,
Throw your head back,
And let My breeze catch you.
You've lost your joy.
Where did it go?
Don't let anything steal it.
It's time to reclaim it today.
Why not right here, right now?
It's time to laugh again."

"You will make known to me the way of life; In Your presence is fullness of joy; In Your right hand there are pleasures forever…"

— Psalm 16:11, NASB

"But those who wait for Yahweh's grace will experience divine strength. They will rise up on soaring wings and fly like eagles, run their race without growing weary, and walk through life without giving up."

— Isaiah 40:31, TPT

"Doors are opening for you
That previously felt shut.
Don't look in the natural,
But trust me!
I'm moving behind the scenes.
I'm making things happen
That you couldn't even do in your own strength.
I'm on the move.
Better get ready."

"Bring the whole tithe into the storehouse, so that there may be food in My house, and put Me to the test now in this," says the Lord of armies, "if I do not open for you the windows of heaven and pour out for you a blessing until it overflows."

— Malachi 3:10, NASB

"Come here and sit on My lap.
Let Me tell you who you are.
Don't let life circumstances define
Who you are.
This is who I say you are.
You were lovingly made by Me.
I thought, 'Ah, today, I know what I'll make,'
And with excitement, I formed you.
I know life's beaten you down a bit,
But listen, that's not who you are.
You were created for greatness.
You are strong.
You are resilient.
You are amazing,
And you can do this!"

"For you know that when your faith is tested it stirs up power within you to endure all things. And then as your endurance grows even stronger it will release perfection into every part of your being until there is nothing missing and nothing lacking."

— JAMES 1:3-4, TPT

"Why do you doubt?
You hear My voice clearly.
I've confirmed to you over and over.
It's now time to act on the word
I spoke to you.
Trust in Me.
Let's do this together.
You're not walking this out alone.
Cast all your fears aside.
Choose trust."

"Trust in the Lord completely, and do not rely on your own opinions. With all your heart rely on Him to guide you, and He will lead you in every decision you make. Become intimate with Him in whatever you do, and He will lead you wherever you go."

— PROVERBS 3:5-6, TPT

13 | I'VE HEARD YOUR PRAYERS

"Let Me breathe hope into you again.
Things might look grim right now.
You've been praying for years for this breakthrough.
'God won't you move,' you cry out.
I've heard your prayers.
Hope again.
I'm coming.
A tidal wave of renewal is coming."

"Therefore prophesy and say to them, 'This is what the Lord God says: 'Behold, I am going to open your graves and cause you to come up out of your graves, My people; and I will bring you into the land of Israel.'"

— EZEKIEL 37:12, NASB

"Let's be honest,
You don't have it all together.
And that's okay!
That's perfect actually!
You need Me.
You can run out on your own but it might hurt.
I'm always going to be right here
Running after you.
Let Me bandage your wounds.
How about you let Me take care of you,
And let's do this together."

"His left hand cradles my head while His right hand holds me close.
I am at rest in this love."

— Song of Songs 2:6, TPT

15 | YOUR DEFENDER

"It's okay to cry.
It's okay to sob.
I'm right here beside you on this floor.
I'm right here beside you,
On My knees holding you.
I will stand in your defense.
I will rise up and protect you,
Against injustice.
You are going to know Me
As your Defender in this season.
I'll rise up on your behalf."

"…but Jesus stooped down and wrote on the ground with His finger…"

— JOHN 8:6, NKJV

"Lately, there's been some confusion
Coming at you from the enemy of this world.
You ask, 'God what is it that I'm really supposed to be doing?
I feel purposeless right now.
Where am I going?'
Listen, it's okay.
You don't have to have it all figured out.
Sometimes, I will just show you the next step.
You may not be able to see the whole path.
But just trust Me
And take the next step I've shown you.
I'll bring the pieces together.
You will someday look back and think,
'Wow, God. You were always right there
Leading me.'"

"And those who know Your name will put their trust in You, For You, Lord, have not abandoned those who seek You."

— PSALM 9:10, NASB

17 | GIVE ME YOUR BURDENS

"I see them.
I know your concerns and worries.
I'm reaching out to them.
Did you know,
I care about them more than you do?
I have a plan for
The people and concerns you carry,
Come in prayer and lay down the burden you're carrying
At my feet.
I've got them.
I really do!"

"Like a shepherd He will tend His flock, In His arm He will gather the lambs And carry them in the fold of His robe..."

— ISAIAH 40:11, NASB

"Did you know,
You don't have to prove your love.
The world will tell you otherwise,
But I'm here to tell you,
You don't have to prove yourself to Me.
There's nothing you could do,
That will make Me think more or less of you.
I'll never revoke or pull back My love from you.
Did you hear me?
I'll never pull back my love from you.
So, quit trying to prove yourself!
Just be."

"There is no power above us or beneath us—no power that could ever be found in the universe that can distance us from God's passionate love, which is lavished upon us through our Lord Jesus, the Anointed One!"

— ROMANS 8:39, TPT

"Come on now.
You're safe.
You're in a safe place with me,
Here in My arms.
Let Me minister to your heart.
You don't have to run.
You don't have to hide.
I see you.
All of you,
And I love you."

"God, you're such a safe and powerful place to find refuge! You're a proven help in time of trouble—more than enough and always available whenever I need you."

— PSALM 46:1, TPT

"Time to get still.
Time to really listen.
Time to put down your agenda
And just be.
Just be.
I'm whispering.
Can you hear me?"

"The Lord will fight for you; you need only to be still."

— Exodus 14:14, NIV

21 | YOU ARE NOT DEFEATED!

"You are not defeated!
Each time the enemy tries to push you down,
You bounce right back up.
'Not today enemy!
You cannot and will not stop me.
I will persevere,' you say.
Don't you know how much I love you?
My strength is made perfect
In your weakness.
I'm fighting for you.
Rise up!
Rise up!
You're not made to stay there.
Rise up!"

"...and I find that the strength of Christ's explosive power infuses me to conquer every difficulty."

— PHILIPPIANS 4:13, TPT

"Take a moment and listen.
I rise up for your defense.
There is healing under my wings.
Come stay close.
Run into Me and
Find your safe place.
I am here.
I haven't gone astray.
Turn to Me,
I want to meet you today.
I'm not a silent God.
I am speaking. Look for Me."

"He who dwells in the secret place of the Most High shall abide under the shadow of the Almighty."

— PSALM 91:1, NKJV

"Offense is not the answer.
Don't let the enemy rob you of your peace.
Let it go.
Lay it down.
Hand it back to Me.
I am working on your behalf."

"A wise person demonstrates patience, for mercy means holding your tongue. When you are insulted, be quick to forgive and forget it, for you are virtuous when you overlook an offense."

— PROVERBS 19:11, TPT

"Leaders,
There are more for you than against you.
Although, it doesn't always feel like that,
Heaven is cheering you on.
Wash away any remnants of challenges and disappointments.
Give your fears to Me.
This is a time to level up.
Who are you really going to look like,
When it rains hardship?
You were made for this.
I don't make mistakes.
I knew you could lead this."

"Do not fear, for I am with you; Do not be afraid, for I am your God. I will strengthen you, I will also help you, I will also uphold you with My righteous right hand."

— ISAIAH 41:10, NASB

"Only be strong and very courageous…"

— JOSHUA 1:7, NASB

"Do you know there is a book in Heaven with your name in it?
From the moment I thought you into existence,
From the very moment I breathed My breath
Into your frame
And created you in your mother's womb,
I knew
You were created for greatness.
I've never doubted you.
I've always seen your potential.
I see what lies ahead in your journey.
Have hope!
You were created to shine."

"So we are convinced that every detail of our lives is continually woven together to fit into God's perfect plan of bringing good into our lives, for we are His lovers who have been called to fulfill His designed purpose."

— ROMANS 8:28, TPT

.

"I make no mistakes.
Everything has been leading up to
This very moment in which you find yourself.
Victory is just around the corner.
Don't bow to fear.
Don't bow to discouragement.
This is your moment.
You were made for this."

"…yet who knows whether you have come to the kingdom for such a time as this?"

— Esther 4:14, NKJV

"Hide yourself in Me.
When you feel weary,
When you feel distracted by the voices in the world,
When you feel discouraged,
Hide yourself in Me.
It's time to get really still,
Dial down,
And listen.
Let Me refresh you
With My sweet presence.
Let Me renew your every thought.
Let Me take the negative ones and replace them with truth.
Time to be still.
Let Me renew you again."

"…arise, my love, my beautiful companion, and run with me to the higher place. For now is the time to arise and come away with me."

— Song of Songs 2:13, TPT

"Hey! I'm knocking!
Are you listening?
I'm trying to catch your attention.
I'm coming with confirmation,
But you're not seeing it.
Have peace on your decision.
Hear My voice;
Go with what I show you."

*"And you will seek Me and find Me when you search for Me with all
your heart."*

— JEREMIAH 29:13, NKJV

29 | DO YOU TRUST ME?

"I never said this 'faith thing' would be easy,
Come on,
It's time to stretch a little higher,
A little wider.
Do you trust Me?
Do you?
Do you really?"

"Now you are ready, my bride, to come with me as we climb the highest peaks together. Come with me through the archway of trust…"

— Song of Songs 4:8, TPT

"Stop engaging in carnal wars,
Petty tensions,
Quarrels,
And misunderstandings.
Stop them . . .
It's only robbing you of your
Peace.
Don't allow any of your precious time,
Energy and emotions
To engage with the enemy's schemes.
Don't allow him to take any territory."

"For we do not wrestle against flesh and blood, but against principalities, against powers, against the rulers of the darkness of this age, against spiritual hosts of wickedness in the heavenly places."

— EPHESIANS 6:12, NKJV

"I see you.
Yeah you!
You who are thinking,
'God doesn't really hear my prayers.'
Yep, I see you.
I know it's hard right now.
I know.
You never thought it would be like this.
I'm gonna pull you through this.
Have hope and joy.
I've got better plans for you."

"I am Yahweh, your mighty God! I grip your right hand and won't let you go! I whisper to you: 'Don't be afraid; I am here to help you!'"

— Isaiah 41:13, TPT

"Today, you need my strength
To face that mountain.
Not in your own strength,
But in mine.
Let's do this together."

"…never turn your gaze from me, for I am your faithful God. I will infuse you with my strength and help you in every situation…"

— Isaiah 41:10, TPT

"Here I come
Running to bring change.
I'm moving in the midst of it all.
I see it
And I know it all.
I'm bringing an answer
And peace
To everything that's trying to steal your faith
In this situation.
I am
A God of hope."

"Can you not discern this new day of destiny breaking forth around you? The early signs of my purposes and plans are bursting forth. The budding vines of new life are now blooming everywhere. The fragrance of their flowers whispers, 'There is change in the air.'"

— SONG OF SONGS 2:13, TPT

"Time to turn about.
Time to wash clean.
Repent,
And sin no more.
It's okay.
I forgive you.
Quit beating yourself up.
Today is a new day.
Let's start over."

"Now Joshua was clothed in filthy garments and was standing before the angel. And he responded and said to those who were standing before him, saying, 'Remove the filthy garments from him.' Again he said to him, 'See, I have taken your guilt away from you and will clothe you with festive robes.'"

— ZECHARIAH 3:3-4, NASB

"Are you hungry for Me?
Are you thirsty for Me?
You can live your day to day
Without me,
But won't live it to the fullest.
I have so much more for you.
Fullness of joy,
Fullness of life,
Fullness of health,
Fullness of peace . . .
The riches of relationship with Me.
So, come
A little closer.
I dare you."

"O God of my life, I'm lovesick for you in this weary wilderness. I thirst with the deepest longings to love you more, with cravings in my heart that can't be described. Such yearning grips my soul for you, my God!"

— PSALM 63:1, TPT

"…but I have come to give you everything in abundance, more than you expect—life in its fullness until you overflow!"

— JOHN 10:10, TPT

"Hear My voice.
Be still for a moment.
I'm speaking.
Ask Me the question,
'God what are You saying right now?'
Open your spiritual ears
I'm speaking."

"But Jesus Himself would often slip away to the wilderness and pray."

— LUKE 5:16, NASB

"Nothing,
Nothing will ever stop Me
From pursuing you!
Why question My hand in your life?
I know,
Right now, it may feel hard to see Me.
It may feel hard to hear Me amidst the chaos,
But I'm right here.
Every step of your journey,
I've been here.
Every valley of disappointment,
Every precipice of joyous moments
I've been here.
I'm not going away.
I'm walking beside you."

"…now He comes closer, even to the places where I hide. He gazes into my soul peering through the portal as He blossoms within my heart. The one I love calls to me."

— Song of Songs 2:9-10, TPT

"Quit comparing yourself.
I think you are amazing!
The enemy is trying to steal your momentum.
Keep your eyesight focused
On what I've assigned for you in this hour.
Don't waste your time
Or give the enemy any ground
To discourage you.
Walk with Me
Hand in hand.
Don't look at what others are doing and get discouraged.
What I've assigned you is impactful.
It will change and shift the atmosphere around you.
It's important for you
To keep your
Focus."

"Stop imitating the ideals and opinions of the culture around you, but be inwardly transformed by the Holy Spirit through a total reformation of how you think. This will empower you to discern God's will as you live a beautiful life, satisfying and perfect in his eyes."

— Romans 12:2, TPT

"Take ten.
Ten minutes to let Me refresh you.
Take a break from the day.
Would you believe that in those ten minutes
Of stillness with Me,
I'll do more with you?
And you'll get more out of this time
Then you've had in a while.
It's an anointed ten minutes.
Come expectant!
Go on!
Set the timer!
I'm coming with a refreshing wind."

"Enter His gates with thanksgiving, And His courtyards with praise. Give thanks to Him, bless His name."

— Psalm 100:4, NASB

"Watch over your reactions.
Reactions to things often
Reveal the condition of your heart.
Today might be challenging to hold your peace.
Agree with Me.
Not today satan!"

"Watch over your heart with all diligence, for from it flow the springs of life."

— PROVERBS 4:23, NASB

"Brush it off!
A spirit of intimidation cannot follow you around any longer!
You are mine.
You are My treasure.
Let no one,
No principality, no schemes of the enemy,
Steal who you are in Me.
And, you have a voice!
It's a voice that's meant to be heard.
In the spirit realm, when you're
Walking in My light,
You are like a wrecking ball
Pushing against darkness.
Time to rise up.
Let nothing intimidate you."

"For the Lord your God is the one who goes with you to fight for you against your enemies to give you victory."

— Deuteronomy 20:4, NIV

"Don't waste your time with distractions.
Follow through with your yes to Me.
Recognize that the enemy tries to combat
Your momentum with Me
Through distractions.
It makes saying 'no,'
Or 'this other project can wait,'
A little easier to say.
Doesn't it?
Follow through with your yes."

"Let your eyes look directly ahead, And let your gaze be fixed straight in front of you. Watch the path of your feet, And all your ways will be established. Do not turn to the right or to the left; Turn your foot from evil."

— PROVERBS 4:25-27, NASB

"Know that every tear you've sown,
Every drop of sweat you've put in,
Every kind word you've released,
Every time you've been My hands and feet
Even when it was inconvenient,
I've seen it.
It will bear fruit.
You will reap the rewards."

*"…for what you plant will always be the very thing you harvest.
The harvest you reap reveals the seed that was planted…"*

— GALATIANS 6:7-8, TPT

"What are you saying about yourself?
What are you saying about your kids or the people
around you?
What are you saying about your future?
Speak My words in faith.
Be careful to release My blessings
And honor from your mouth.
If only you could see the power your words have.
Game changer."

"Then God said, 'Let there be light'; and there was light."

— GENESIS 1:3, NASB

"You will also declare a thing, And it will be established for you; So light will shine on your ways."

— JOB 22:28, NKJV

"Come take a break with Me.
Come sit here with Me
Under My apple tree.
Lean your head
Against My chest,
And allow Me to minister to you
Here in this place of rest.
Draw away with Me."

"My beloved is to me the most fragrant apple tree—He stands above the sons of men. Sitting under His grace-shadow, I blossom in His shade, enjoying the sweet taste of His pleasant, delicious fruit, resting with delight where His glory never fades."

— Song of Songs 2:3, TPT

"Imagine how kids swing.
Often, they'll lean back,
Way back,
Put their head back,
And allow the sun to beam down on their face.
Giggling,
Their joy refreshes the air.
They're in the moment,
Experiencing life vivaciously,
Taking their world in.
Letting go of their cares,
And enjoying Me.
Try it out.
Let down your guard
And come swing."

"For I give plenty of water to the weary ones, and refresh everyone who languishes."

— JEREMIAH 31:25, NASB

47 | **NEW BLUEPRINTS**

"Okay.
So that didn't work out as you thought it would.
It's okay.
Let's start over.
Come back to the drawing board with Me,
And let's draw up new plans,
New sketches,
New dreams.
You might be surprised
That these new blueprints
Will be better than before."

"Write the vision And make it plain on tablets, That he may run who reads it. For the vision is yet for an appointed time; But at the end it will speak, and it will not lie. Though it tarries, wait for it; Because it will surely come, It will not tarry."

— Habakkuk 2:2-3, NKJV

"You're not a quitter!
You're a fighter,
One who perseveres,
A survivor,
A keeps-getting-up-er,
A never-stops-er!
Don't stop now.
Don't waste your time looking back in regret.
Keep moving forward.
Keep going.
You've got this."

"…and let us run with perseverance the race marked out for us, fixing our eyes on Jesus, the pioneer and perfecter of faith…"

— Hebrews 12:1-2, NIV

"Ever wonder if My timing is off?
It can feel like: 'Why Now Lord?'
Why, of all the times would You allow
This to happen right now?'
Won't you trust Me?
I see the big picture.
My timing is always right."

"For I know the plans that I have for you,' declares the Lord, 'plans for prosperity and not for disaster, to give you a future and a hope. Then you will call upon Me and come and pray to Me, and I will listen to you."

— JEREMIAH 29:11-12, NASB

"Don't forget to play.
To My hard worker:
I love how diligent you are.
Don't forget
I created you to enjoy My goodness!
Don't forget to play hard too.
Pour out hard,
Refresh
And do something that brings you
Joy today."

"It is a sign between Me and the children of Israel forever; for in six days the Lord made the heavens and the earth, and on the seventh day He rested and was refreshed."

— Exodus 31:17, NKJV

"I'm standing up on your behalf.
I am a God of justice.
I will set the wrong things right.
Press into Me right now.
Abide in Me.
Let Me be your defender.
I stand up for the defenseless.
Let Me be your voice."

"Who made heaven and earth, The sea, and all that is in them; Who keeps truth forever, Who executes justice for the oppressed, Who gives food to the hungry. The Lord gives freedom to the prisoners. The Lord opens the eyes of the blind; The Lord raises those who are bowed down; The Lord loves the righteous."

— PSALM 146:6-8, NKJV

"There's a plan in it all.
You can't see how,
But someday you'll look back
At this very moment,
And see My hand
In it all."

"For My eyes are on all their ways; they are not hidden from My face, nor is their iniquity hidden from My eyes."

— JEREMIAH 16:17, NKJV

"Pick up your pen and dream again.
Begin to write down your goals,
Visions,
And dreams you have.
Now think of something that's beyond your
Visions, hopes and dreams that you wrote down.
Ask Me for an impossibility.
Begin to dream at that level of faith.
I'm stretching you.
No great man or woman
Who changed history,
Did it out of their own strength or vision.
Ask Me for the impossible.
Believe in something so much bigger than you.
Man is limited, but I have no limits."

"...for assuredly, I say to you, if you have faith as a mustard seed, you will say to this mountain, 'Move from here to there,' and it will move; and nothing will be impossible for you."

— MATTHEW 17:20, NASB

"Doubt and fear
Are your two biggest inhibitors right now.
What are you afraid of really?
Are you afraid of what people might think?
Are you afraid of failing?
Are you afraid of the risk involved?
Are you afraid of what it might cost you?
Fear is not of Me.
That's not the breath of Heaven,
Rather, the breath of the enemy
Whispering in your ear.
Do you doubt that you've heard Me correctly?
Do you doubt yourself?
I'm right here. I've given you the vision.
I've given you the direction.
Now it's up to you to walk it out.
Choose to crush fear and doubt
Under your feet today."

*"But let him ask in faith, with no doubting, for he who doubts is like
a wave of the sea driven and tossed by the wind."*

— JAMES 1:6, NKJV

"Refreshing winds of Heaven
Blow down now.
I'm giving you a new perspective.
Fresh eyes to see.
I grant you the ability to come up higher
And truly see what I see."

"...and behold, a door standing open in heaven. And the first voice which I heard was like a trumpet speaking with me, saying, 'Come up here, and I will show you things which must take place after this.'"

— REVELATION 4:1, NKJV

"Catch those little thoughts.
Those little whispers
That criticize, judge and condemn.
I'm for you,
Not against you.
My love covers all.
Who are you listening to today?"

"You must catch the troubling foxes, those sly little foxes that hinder our relationship. For they raid our budding vineyard of love to ruin what I've planted within you. Will you catch them and remove them for me? We will do it together."

— SONG OF SONGS 2:15, TPT

57 | WAIT FOR MY PERFECT TIMING

"Don't rush ahead of My timing.
Wait, have patience.
Know that I have the best in store for you.
Wait for My best.
Wait for My peace.
Don't sell yourself short
Of my very best for your destiny.
Don't you know
That I love you so much
That I will give you the best?"

"There is an appointed time for everything. And there is a time for every matter under heaven—"

— Ecclesiastes 3:1, NASB

"Why not?
Listen, the world will tell you
All the reasons and answers to the question
'Why not.'
Dream big.
The naysayers
Are always there,
Trying to steal your passion,
Your vision, your faith
The doubters
And the reasons to stop dreaming
Will never leave.
They will only increase,
As your faith takes you higher.
The negative voices will only grow louder
As you take on new territory with Me.
As you press forward in faith,
It's going to take tenacity and perseverance.
It will require you to stand your ground in faith.
I am the Lion of Judah
And I'm roaring on your behalf.
I shut the mouth of the enemy now
For taking you off your course.
I speak the truth.
You can do this!
We can do this!
You were created for this.

Keep going.
Keep dreaming.
Keep planting.
Keep taking steps forward in faith.
And watch the mountains I'll move."

"I will give you the keys of the kingdom of heaven; and whatever you bind on earth shall have been bound in heaven, and whatever you loose on earth shall have been loosed in heaven."

— MATTHEW 16:19, NASB

"Time to rise up in your discernment.
Who is carrying My voice in this hour?
Who is pointing you toward Me?
Who is reflecting My nature?
Use wisdom.
Use discernment.
Remain in Me."

"Abide in Me, and I in you. As the branch cannot bear fruit of itself, unless it abides in the vine, neither can you, unless you abide in Me. I am the vine, you are the branches. He who abides in Me, and I in him, bears much fruit; for without Me you can do nothing."

— JOHN 15:4-5, NKJV

"I have a new direction for you,
Like a sailboat that catches a new wind,
That is forced to recalibrate and shift.
That is where you are right now.
Don't worry.
I'm behind it.
I am blowing all things
Into place for this change.
I speak peace over your adjustment.
Trust Me in the new."

"And we know that God causes all things to work together for good to those who love God, to those who are called according to His purpose."

— ROMANS 8:28, NASB

"It's time to dance again.
You've lost your joy.
Exhaustion has taken over.
Would you believe Me?
I'm giving you a new song.
I'm giving you a new name.
It's time to get your dance back."

"Go ahead—sing your brand-new song to the Lord! He is famous for His miracles and marvels, for He is victorious through His mighty power and holy strength."

— PSALM 98:1, TPT

"I'm restoring you.
Your name
Your family
Your finances
Your health
Your joy
Your peace
Your work
Your value
Your destiny
Your calling
Your vision
Your purpose
Your home
Your freedom.
Breathe again.
I'm your Restorer!"

"A lion has roared! Who will not fear? The Lord God has spoken! Who can do anything but prophesy?"

— Amos 3:8, NASB

"You're not drowning.
Come swim in My presence.
Everything is trying to steal your
Very ability to
Lift your head
And breathe through it all.
I'm releasing the ability to
Navigate through it all.
My compass is peace.
I will make a way where there is no way."

"Stand firm therefore, having belted your waist with truth, and having put on the breastplate of righteousness, and having strapped on your feet the preparation of the gospel of peace; in addition to all, taking up the shield of faith with which you will be able to extinguish all the flaming arrows of the evil one. And take the helmet of salvation and the sword of the Spirit, which is the word of God."

— EPHESIANS 6:14-17, NASB

"Rest your mind.
You don't have to have it
All figured out.
I'm just showing you
The next step for now.
Rest
In
That."

"Within your heart you can make plans for your future, but the Lord chooses the steps you take to get there."

— Proverbs 16:9, TPT

"I'm restoring your relationships.
Bringing healing to old bridges
That seem precarious.
Let Me show you friendships
With the right people
To run with in this season.
People who will encourage you
On the right path.
People who will correct you in love.
People who have your back
No matter the cost.
You weren't meant to do this life alone.
You have Me, but I'm also
Sending you helpers.
I will show you who is safe,
Who to trust and who to let in.
Let Me heal your heart today
Of past relationships gone wrong.
I'm doing something new."

"Always be humble and gentle. Be patient with each other, making allowance for each other's faults because of your love. Make every effort to keep yourselves united in the Spirit, binding yourselves together with peace."

— EPHESIANS 4:2-3, NLT

"I see your heart.
With tenderness, I care for it.
I see the inner desires of your heart,
The things nobody knows.
Even the small things
That you don't want to ask Me for,
Because in the grand scheme of things,
You think they don't matter.
I see them.
You matter to Me.
Every drop of blood I shed for you,
Means I value your heart and your desires.
Don't you see? Your heart is a treasure!"

"Never doubt God's mighty power to work in you and accomplish all this. He will achieve infinitely more than your greatest request, your most unbelievable dream, and exceed your wildest imagination! He will outdo them all, for his miraculous power constantly energizes you."

— EPHESIANS 3:20, TPT

"May your emotions
Be at peace.
May every thought
Bring you peace.
Just take a breath.
Go on.
Really do it.
Just breathe.
There.
Isn't that better?"

"…then He got up and rebuked the winds and the sea, and it became perfectly calm."

— Matthew 8:26, NASB

"You think that every door
Has been shut,
But the right door is
being opened.
Perhaps walking through it,
Means catching the vision, or
Bringing someone else into the picture to help.
The door is there
If you just ask Me
And look for it."

"Blessed is the person who listens to me, watching daily at my gates, waiting at my doorposts."

— PROVERBS 8:34, NASB

"I've known every step you would take.
I've known
Every time you would fall and need to get back up.
I've known every right turn you would take,
I've known every wrong turn.
I've known you from the beginning.
I know where you are going.
You may think that I feel distant, but
I've been here all along.
I'm not a distant, and uncaring Father.
No . . . no!
I'm always near.
I've picked you up every time.
I've helped you along the way even when you
Couldn't see Me.
I'm right here."

"You enlarge my steps under me, And my feet have not slipped."

— PSALM 18:36, NASB

"Find me.
Find Me in the busyness of the day.
Find Me in the chaos and messes.
Find Me in the pressure and deadlines.
Find Me in the confrontations
That are sometimes unpleasant.
Find Me
In all that you juggle.
I'm in it all."

"Be still, and know that I am God…"

— Psalm 46:10, NKJV

"You and I are walking
Hand in hand.
You and I are walking in the new land.
It's uncharted,
And a bit messy.
A bit different than what you thought.
See through My eyes.
The purpose is there.
See with My eyes of potential.
You'll get there."

"So He said, 'I will certainly be with you…'"

— Exodus 3:12, NKJV

"Reach deep, deep down,
And see what I'm uncovering
that still needs healing.
I died on that cross
And resurrected,
So that
You can walk
In wholeness.
Bring before Me, every insecurity, wound and pain,
Every doubt, and frustration.
Let Me heal it for you.
Hand them over to Me.
I took them for you on the cross.
Day by day, you are starting to
Look more like Me,
Let's walk together."

"For I am confident of this very thing, that He who began a good work among you will complete it by the day of Christ Jesus."

— Philippians 1:6, NASB

"I'm going to give you
The right words to say today.
Wisdom and grace in conversations.
Today, you will feel
My Holy Spirit
Using your words
To reflect Me.
Let Me open your mouth,
Fill it with My presence
And pour out
My hope
Onto others around you."

"But the Lord said to him, 'Who has made the human mouth? Or who makes anyone unable to speak or deaf, or able to see or blind? Is it not I, the Lord? Now then go, and I Myself will be with your mouth, and instruct you in what you are to say.'"

— Exodus 4:11-12, NASB

"You're overthinking things too much.
Just jump with raw obedience
Into what I've shown you.
Don't get stuck on the
'What if's'.
I'll show you
What you need along the way.
Just trust Me
In this next step."

"Now when He had finished speaking, He said to Simon, 'Put out into the deep water and let down your nets for a catch.' Simon responded and said, 'Master, we worked hard all night and caught nothing, but I will do as You say and let down the nets.' And when they had done this, they caught a great quantity of fish, and their nets began to tear; so they signaled to their partners in the other boat to come and help them. And they came and filled both of the boats, to the point that they were sinking."

— LUKE 5:4-7, NASB

"Time to grow.
Time to expand.
Time to stretch.
Time to run forward
In full faith
That
I'll catch you."

"Enlarge the place of your tent; Stretch out the curtains of your dwellings, do not spare them; Lengthen your ropes And strengthen your pegs."

— Isaiah 54:2, NASB

"Hear that?
Those are the sounds of Heaven.
The sounds of Heaven invading your space,
Invading your circumstance,
Invading your very day.
The veil is much thinner than you think.
I'm looking right at you.
My very eyes are upon you, and
I'm so proud.
What you don't know,
Is how many times a day
I look at you and say
'Wow! Did you see what my kid just did?'
I'm that close."

"When Solomon had finished praying, fire came down from heaven and consumed the burnt offering and the sacrifices; and the glory of the Lord filled the temple. And the priests could not enter the house of the Lord, because the glory of the Lord had filled the Lord's house. When all the children of Israel saw how the fire came down, and the glory of the Lord on the temple, they bowed their faces to the ground on the pavement, and worshiped and praised the Lord, saying: 'For He is good, For His mercy endures forever.'"

— 2 CHRONICLES 7:1-3, NKJV

"Have courage today.
Look at that mountain square on
And command it to move.
No more trudging.
Today believe with all your might,
And all your faith
That this mountain is falling down.
Nothing's standing in your way.
Acceleration."

"Now it came about on the third day that Esther put on her royal robes and stood in the inner courtyard of the king's palace in front of the king's rooms, and the king was sitting on his royal throne in the throne room, opposite the entrance to the palace. When the king saw Esther the queen standing in the courtyard, she obtained favor in his sight; and the king extended to Esther the golden scepter which was in his hand…"

— ESTHER 5:1-2, NASB

"Everything the enemy
Has stolen from you,
I'm returning to you.
Do you believe Me in that?
Declare with Me in that.
Thank you, Jesus
That you are
Returning my . . . today!"

"The Lord also restored the fortunes of Job when he prayed for his friends, and the Lord increased double all that Job had."

— JOB 42:10, NASB

"Worship will break the warfare
You're going through right now.
Worship cuts through and cleans up the atmosphere.
The demons flee at the sound of My name,
At the sound of your worship.
Yes, your worship!
You may think,
'But God, I'm not some anointed psalmist.'
Listen, it doesn't matter.
Just worship. Sing praise!
Whatever comes to mind.
Sing thanksgiving and watch the enemy run!"

"When they began singing and praising, the Lord set ambushes against the sons of Ammon, Moab, and Mount Seir, who had come against Judah; so they were struck down."

— 2 CHRONICLES 20:22, NASB

"Leaders, I'm renewing your strength.
You carve paths
Where there are no ways or there are blockages.
You see the bigger picture
And encourage people along.
You sacrifice everything
When no one is looking.
You persevere
Even when you may feel discouraged.
You press into Me as your strength in everything.
You don't give up
When others may tell you to take an easier way.
You maintain your focus and your stance of faith.
You are changing the world for Me,
One day at a time.
I'm renewing you."

"So I sent messengers to them, saying, 'I am doing a great work and am unable to come down. Why should the work stop while I leave it and come down to you?'"

— NEHEMIAH 6:3, NASB

"Every drop of blood,
Every bit of My torn flesh,
Every tear that I shed,
Was worth it for you.
Don't you see?
You're My treasure.
You were the joy set before Me.
I had you in My vision
As I walked to that cross.
I had you in My vision
As I faced betrayal
And the rejection of many.
You were worth it.
Don't you ever forget it."

"Then, looking into Thomas' eyes, He said, 'Put your finger here in the wounds of my hands. Here—put your hand into my wounded side and see for yourself. Thomas, don't give in to your doubts any longer, just believe!'"

— JOHN 20:27, TPT

"I'm bringing streams
to the dry places in your life.
You know those places.
The ones that feel like,
'Where are you God?
I thought you were the
God of breakthrough?
Breakthrough
Would be really nice right now!'
I am coming
To renew your hope,
Restore your heart,
And restore your faith
In Me.
I'm moving."

*"I am doing something brand new, something unheard of. Even now
it sprouts and grows and matures. Don't you perceive it? I will make
a way in the wilderness and open up flowing streams in the desert."*

— ISAIAH 43:19, TPT

"Here I am.
Leading you,
Guiding you.
Today,
I want you to
Try something new.
Trust Me.
Really
Trust Me."

"Become intimate with Him in whatever you do, and He will lead you wherever you go."

— Proverbs 3:6, TPT

"Ask Me for more!
Go On!
Do it!
I dare you.
Today, I'm opening your eyes
To see,
And opening your ears to hear.
I'm removing the blockages
That were there,
So that you can hear clearly.
Go on,
Ask Me the question
That's been weighing in your heart.
I've got an answer."

"Now we're no longer living like slaves under the law, but we enjoy being God's very own sons and daughters! And because we're His, we can access everything our Father has—for we are heirs of God through Jesus, the Messiah!"

— GALATIANS 4:7, TPT

"Interruptions of peace.
Sounds like an oxymoron, right?
Today, I'm going to provide
You with invasions of
Peaceful moments
Amidst the chaos,
To connect your heart to Me.
Watch for Me."

"Now when it was evening on that day, the first day of the week, and when the doors were shut where the disciples were together due to fear of the Jews, Jesus came and stood in their midst, and said to them, 'Peace be to you.'"

— JOHN 20:19, NASB

"Just
be with Me.
Lay down
Your way of getting there.
Just be.
Let Me soak you with My presence,
As if you were
Floating underwater,
Under the weight
Of My heavy presence,
Looking right up
Into My eyes.
Peace,
Be still.
Let Me fill you."

"...come walk with me as you walked with Adam in your paradise
garden. Come taste the fruits of your life in me."

— SONG OF SONGS 4:16, TPT

"There's a shift in the wind.
Can you feel that?
Those are the winds of peace.
Every weapon that the enemy has
Formed against you in this very moment,
Is being destroyed.
Every demonic strong tower that stands against you,
Must come down.
Every attack or arrow
That is trying to bring disarray
In your life,
Is being intercepted
And stopped
By angels that I've released.
I am for you.
I speak to your storm,
'Peace, be still.'"

"Behold, I have given you authority to walk on snakes and scorpions, and authority over all the power of the enemy, and nothing will injure you."

— LUKE 10:19, NASB

"I am calling forth a spring
Where there has been a drought in your life.
A drought of encouragement,
A drought of support,
A drought of love,
A drought of health and wholeness,
A drought of finances,
A drought of good leadership,
A drought of friendship,
A drought of faith,
A drought of vision to see beyond,
A drought of momentum,
A drought of passion,
A drought of joy.
I'm bringing my refreshing spring of hope,
My refreshing spring of healing.
Refreshing nourishment found in My presence."

"For the Lord your God is bringing you into a good land, a land of streams of water, of fountains and springs, flowing out in valleys and hills…"

— Deuteronomy 8:7, NASB

"You have a calling!
There's a unique destiny that I have for you.
You see, there's no one in the world quite like you.
With your unique gift mix, quirks and talents,
You are destined for greatness!
So please,
Stop trying to be someone or something
That you're not.
You being you,
Is the best thing you can offer this world.
Step into your calling.
Self-acceptance is such a key."

"For You created my innermost parts; You wove me in my mother's womb. I will give thanks to You, because I am awesomely and wonderfully made; Wonderful are Your works, And my soul knows it very well. My frame was not hidden from You When I was made in secret, And skillfully formed in the depths of the earth; Your eyes have seen my formless substance; And in Your book were written All the days that were ordained for me, When as yet there was not one of them."

— PSALM 139:13-16, NASB

"I'm waiting
For you to
Set your own will aside.
It goes so much better
When we do this together.
Your own strength
Will eventually take you
To burn out.
Let Me help you.
Let Me carry your burdens.
Let Me show you the way.
Let Me fill the gaps
And the spaces
Toward that goal.
Let's do this
Together."

"For with God nothing will be impossible."

— Luke 1:37, NKJV

"Cry out to Me,
And I will
Come to you.
Every time,
When all hope is gone,
I am here.
I hear your plea.
I hear that request.
I'm sending the answer."

"I cried out to you in my distress, the delivering God, and from your temple-throne you heard my troubled cry. My sobs came right into your heart and you turned your face to rescue me."

— PSALM 18:6, TPT

"Pruning seasons aren't fun.
As I pull back layers
Of your heart that still need healing,
That still need correction,
Know that
I'm pruning you out of love.
For growth to come,
There must be pruning.
For new life to come forth,
There must be a
Dying to self.
Hang in there.
Allow Me to go a little deeper,
So that
I may bring you
Into full fruition."

"…the season for singing and pruning the vines has arrived. I hear the cooing of doves in our land, filling the air with songs to awaken you and guide you forth."

— Song of Songs 2:12, TPT

"Reach up
And pull down from Heaven today!
It's okay,
Go ahead and ask.
What is it you need?
You're my daughter.
You're my son.
You can approach Me
And
Just ask."

"And I will give you the keys of the kingdom of heaven, and whatever you bind on earth will be bound in heaven, and whatever you loose on earth will be loosed in heaven."

— Matthew 16:19, NKJV

"The Lion of Judah roars,
And silences the voice of the enemy.
How dare he?
How dare the devil try to steal from you
Who I say you are?
Every lie, every form of malice
Must bow down now
Under My feet.
I am speaking over you
That you are My son,
You are My daughter.
You are an heir to My kingdom.
You have purpose, you have destiny.
You have days ahead of you to fulfill.
You have a place
At the banquet table.
You have a place in the Kingdom."

"You prepare a table before me in the presence of my enemies; You have anointed my head with oil; My cup overflows."

— Psalm 23:5, NASB

"This is just training ground
For the rest of your life.
The lessons you are walking through
And learning now,
You will someday use in Heaven.
I am training you
To reign.
So, take a moment
And reflect.
What am I training you in now?
Where have you grown?"

"Blessed is a man who perseveres under trial; for once he has been approved, he will receive the crown of life which the Lord has promised to those who love Him."

— JAMES 1:12, NASB

"Did you know,
I really like you?
I do!
Of course, I love you,
But I really like you.
I enjoy who you are.
The funny way you do things sometimes,
Your strengths
and frailties.
I really do enjoy you.
Do you
Enjoy you?
Because you should.
I created you."

"Then the Lord God formed the man of dust from the ground and breathed into his nostrils the breath of life; and the man became a living person."

— Genesis 2:7, NASB

"My stamp of approval
Is on you.
As you remain in Me
You will accelerate.
What I have planned,
Nothing can stand against.
That is your inheritance.
Now go
Take hold of it.
Claim what is already yours."

"…but those who wait for the Lord, they will inherit the land."

— PSALM 37:9, NASB

•

"Clarity from confusion.
Ever feel like there's a swarm of fog
Over you
Blocking you from being able to
Hear Me or see Me?
I'm breaking a spirit of confusion off of you
That the enemy's assigned
To attack you in this season.
The fog's lifting.
The clarity is coming.
Hear My voice again."

"Your ears will hear a word behind you, saying, 'This is the way, walk in it,' whenever you turn to the right or to the left."

— Isaiah 30: 21, NASB

"Listen
Just be still now and really listen.
Nope, be more still than that.
Quiet down your thoughts and emotions,
And really listen.
It's important in this season
That you close off voices that don't speak
My truth
Into your life.
You are on the brink of breakthrough.
At this time, the enemy tries to
Bring confusion
To throw you off.
Now, you need to remain steadfast,
And only allow
Voices of faith
To speak into your life and encourage you.
Let me encourage you.
You are that close! Hold on now!
Hold onto faith."

"Therefore, my beloved brothers and sisters, be firm, immovable, always excelling in the work of the Lord, knowing that your labor is not in vain in the Lord."

— 1 Corinthians 15:58, NASB

"The very place where you feel the
Most broken,
Will be your greatest triumph.
The threshing floor
Will teach you many things.
The greatest fruit
Will pour out
Of this pressing.
Through this process,
You will help many
Along the way.
No tear is shed
That I don't catch.
I'm right beside you through this.
We'll get through it.
I haven't forgotten you."

*"…behold, like the clay in the potter's hand, so are you in My hand,
house of Israel."*

— JEREMIAH 18:6, NASB

SALVATION PRAYER

Lord,

I confess that I am a sinner. I don't have it all together and I need you Jesus in my life. Please forgive me of my sins.

Jesus I believe that you died on the cross for me. Through your resurrection on the cross, I may have eternal life with you.

Would you come into my life now, as my Lord and Savior. Would you come into my heart. I surrender the leadership of my life to you.

Thank you Jesus.

Now Lord, would you please fill me with Your Holy Spirit who will guide me and show me your ways.

In Jesus' name. Amen.

  *If you prayed this prayer, please contact us at info@anawerner.org

Guess what? Today is an exciting day! Today is the start of your NEW LIFE in Christ!! Your name is now written in the book of life in Heaven!! HALLELUJAH!

MEET THE AUTHOR

ANA WERNER and her husband Sam currently reside in Kansas City, Missouri. They have two precious kids who keep them busy. Collectively they have ministered in over thirteen different nations overseas. They were both called by God for missions and ministry at a young age.

Ana moves in the prophetic and healing gifts. She is a Seer and teaches on seeing in the Supernatural with Jesus in churches and arenas around the world. Ana is an inspiring author and speaker. Her transparency as she shares on the realities and experiences, she has in Heaven, always bring Holy Spirit and the power of God into the room when she speaks. Healing, signs and wonders follow her ministry.

She writes, "My deepest desire by sharing about Heaven is for people to grow more in love with Jesus, step into freedom, and live life to its fullest for Him! He is worth all our love! Intimacy with Him brings healing, healing brings freedom, and freedom brings joy!"

To find about more about the author and other books she has written, please visit her online:

🌐 www.**ANAWERNER**.org

Printed in Great Britain
by Amazon

18042549R10125